Cut Paper, Silhouettes, and Stencils

An Instruction Book

Christian Rubi

Cut Paper
Silhouettes
and Stencils

An Instruction Book

Translated by Alba Lorman

KAYE & WARD/London
VAN NOSTRAND REINHOLD COMPANY/New York

CONTENTS

Van Nostrand Reinhold Company Regional Offices:
New York Cincinnati Chicago Millbrae Dallas

The Swiss edition of this book, *Papierschnitt Scherenschnitt Schablonenschnitt*,
Copyright © 1970 by Büchler-Verlag Wabern
This edition published in the United States in 1972 by
Van Nostrand Reinhold Company
A Division of Litton Educational Publishing, Inc.
450 West 33rd Street, New York, N.Y. 10001
and in Great Britain in 1972 by
Kaye & Ward Ltd.
194–200 Bishopsgate
London E.C.2

Library of Congress Catalog Card Number: 73–150728
ISBN 0 7182 0793 9

Printed in Switzerland

Paper Cutting

Cutting pictures from paper is an ancient art. It was cultivated especially during the eleventh century by the well-known shadow theaters of the Orient. We are told that in Turkey during the sixteenth century there was a craft guild of those "who made all sorts of carved work of paper." In 1582, as the guilds of Constantinople solemnly filed past the sultan, the paper carvers exhibited "a very beautiful garden and a castle decorated with flowers made of multicolored papers, artistically carved." At that time knives and not scissors were used for carving these works of art.

European painters of the Gothic period also used paper cutting. The ornamental borders around the paintings on the walls of Gothic churches were done with folded stencils. Choir stalls built in Switzerland before the Reformation were occasionally decorated with stencil paintings. Later on, these examples were adapted for adorning furniture and household utensils.

During the seventeenth century, chests in farm houses were usually beautified with stencil paintings. Rural artists also knew how to cut paper. They took their examples from works by painters in the large cities, who were in turn inspired by Renaissance works. Since folded cuts were used, these ornaments were divided symmetrically and, therefore, well balanced.

During the eighteenth century, the preference was for colorful floral ornamentation, and stencil painting disappeared. However, paper cutting was still used for ornamentation. Up to the middle of the last century, paper cuts were used as borders, backgrounds for decorative lettering on birth certificates, declarations of love, New Year's wishes, and religious texts. With the aid of a well-ground penknife, notaries and executors of legal documents designed attractive paper ornaments for use on book covers and as seals. Blacksmiths and locksmiths also used folded cuts as patterns for door knockers and door plates.

Paper cutting will provide you with many hours of continuous enjoyment. Very little material is required. Paper should be neither too thin nor too thick. The type of knife I recommend is a mat knife, which is sold in most artist supply stores.

WHY THIS PARTICULAR KNIFE?

1. Its handle best fits the shape of the hand.
2. The steel is neither too hard nor too soft.
3. The shape of the blade is exactly right for cutting paper.
4. It is inexpensive.

SHARPEN THE MAT KNIFE BEFORE USING IT!

Knife sharpening is child's play for those who know that the blade of a knife is actually a wedge and that the sides should be as close to each other as possible so that the wedge can enter the material easily. The four drawings below demonstrate the following:
1. A cutting wedge that is too wide.
2. A slimmer, better cutting wedge.
3. A wedge that has become blunted with use.
4. A close-up of the blunted edge.

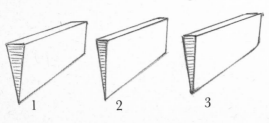
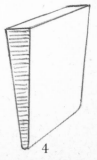

The next three drawings show the right way and the wrong way to resharpen the wedge.

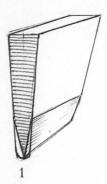  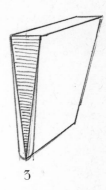

1   2   3

1. The blade has been pressed too hard on the cutting edge while sharpening. Its bottom now corresponds to a wider wedge. Even if the cutting edge were sharpened, it would be much harder to penetrate wood or paper.
2. What has just been explained applies even more in this diagram because the edges meet at a very obtuse angle.
3. The blade here has been evenly sharpened from top to bottom and the original pointed angle of the sides has been maintained.

HOW TO SHARPEN THE MAT KNIFE

1. Fold a hand-sized piece of fine sandpaper or emery cloth in half (rough side out).
2. Put this in front of you, on the edge of a table.
3. Press the knife blade flat on the sandpaper, the back of the blade in front, and move from one end to the other. Exert a little more pressure on the cutting edge than on the back edge, but not so much that the back is no longer touching the base. Repeat this several times.
4. Then turn the knife to the other side and repeat the same sharpening procedure.
5. By gently sliding your thumb along the inside you can test the cutting edge for sharpness. If it is not sharp enough, start all over again.
6. A final sharpness is obtained by polishing the blade on a newspaper. This is done in the same manner as described above.

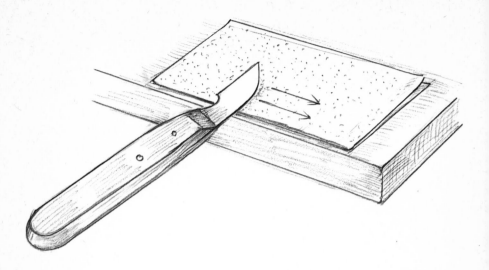

Guard against applying special pressure when sharpening toward the tip! If the tip becomes somewhat rounded in time, the back of the knife should be filed. To do this, press the knife against the edge of a table as shown in the diagram below, and shorten the blade with a triangular or flat file until the tip is sufficiently pointed.

The success of paper cutting depends on a properly prepared knife tip.

Important! Paper should be folded very neatly and hard. Flatten the edges properly with a creaser or some similar tool.

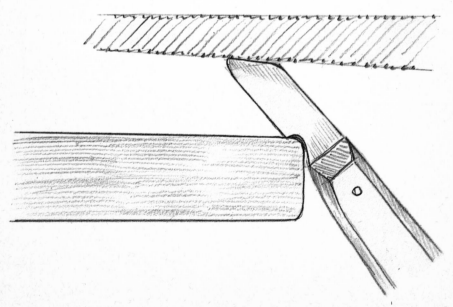

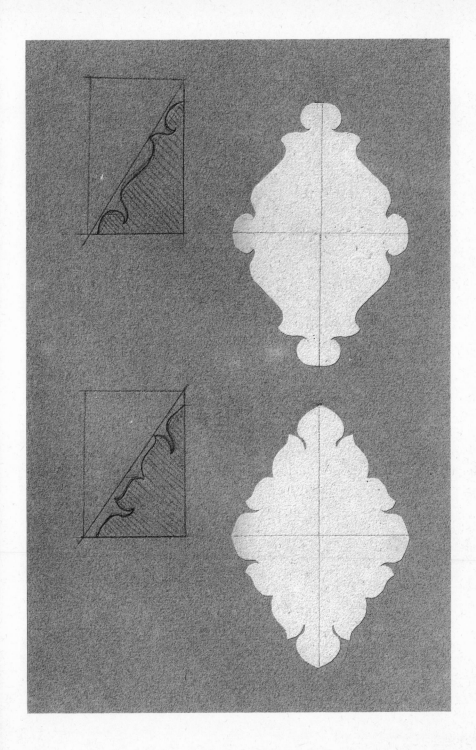

Fold a rectangular piece of paper crosswise. Draw notches along the diagonal. Use cardboard underneath as a support.

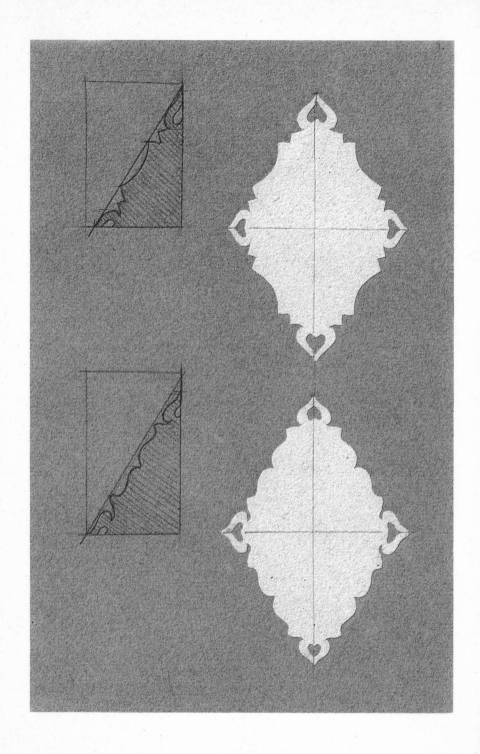

Double-folded paper cut differently. At the four corners are heart-shaped sections.

Draw two circles on square of paper and fold through the center.

Pattern for a door knocker, from the Rectory of the minister of Lauenen, near Saanen, 1734. Design is made with a quadruplefold cut. Fold accurately, securing loose ends with adhesive tape. Circular opening is cut out with a round chisel.

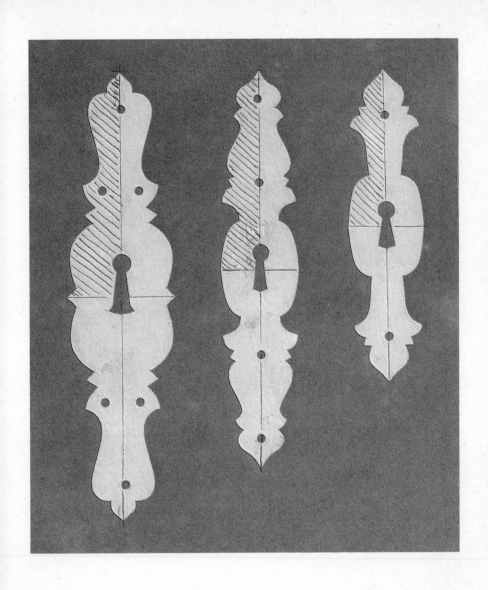

Designs for door plates were double-folded.

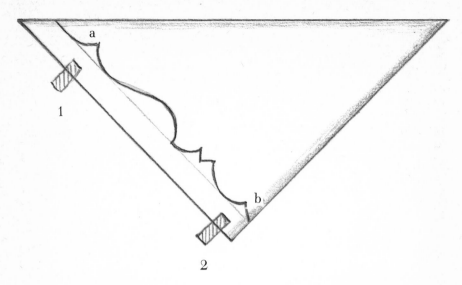

To make an eightfold cut, fold paper three times. Put adhesive tapes over loose edges (1 and 2). Draw these two cuts (*a* and *b*) last.

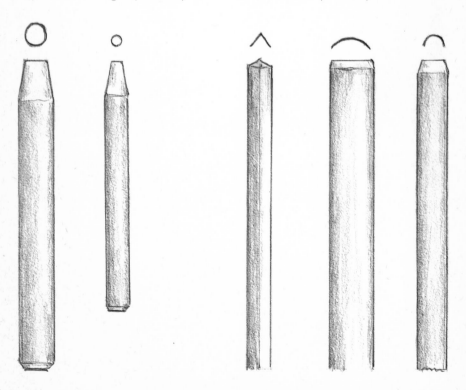

Left: Two leather punches. Right: Three awls. Such tools are very useful for the eightfold cut. Certain shapes can be punched out by hammering on the vertically held tool. Use cardboard support underneath.

Religious sayings from Grison, 1778. Eightfold cut.

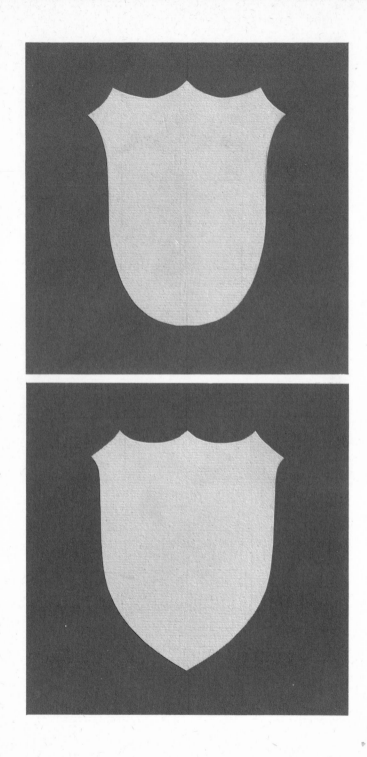

Shapes of coats of arms. Single folds.

Coats of arms, richly decorated.

Heart shapes. Single folds along broadsides.

Heart shapes with additional decoration.

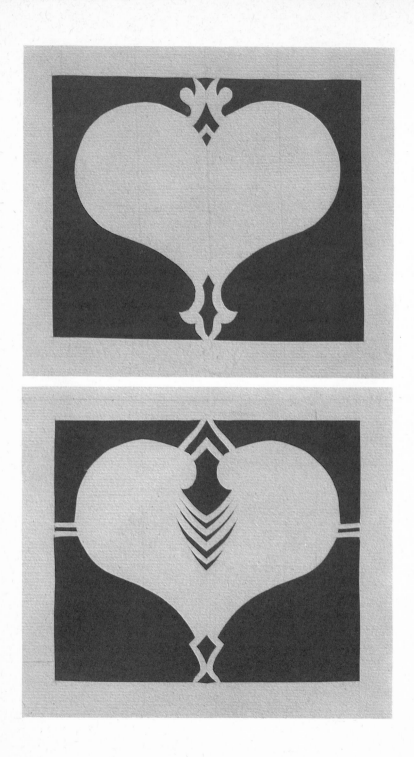

Heart shapes, suspended within a rectangle. Bottoms are connected to the frame by cross pieces.

Heart shape, fixed to the frame with decorative stays.

With ornamental additions, the heart shape can also be made to decorate
an upright rectangle.

24

Floral ornaments can be used for anchorage instead of stays.

Decorative scrolls follow the heart shape.

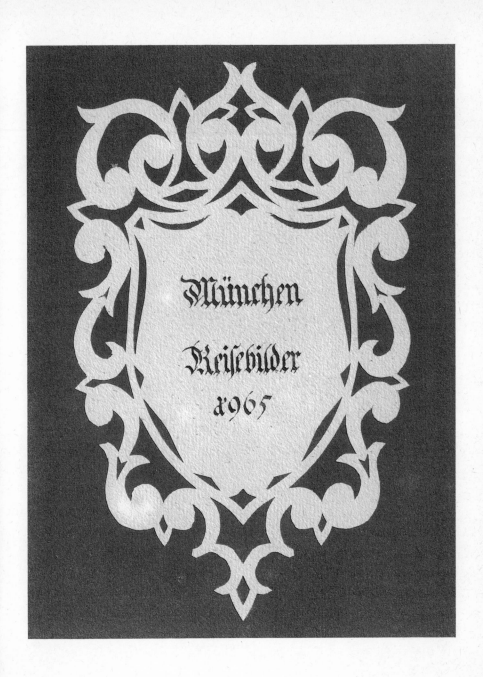

Design for opening page of a photo album.

Another design for a photo album. Cover the writing with clear lacquer before pasting it on.

An engagement greeting. Cut out the heart shape first, then the birds. Start first with the bodies, then wings and heads, and lastly do the claws and beaks.

Experiment with birds and a heart-shaped ornament, attached to the frame without stays.

These bird shapes touch the frame in many places. These are extremely
useful exercises to do.

31

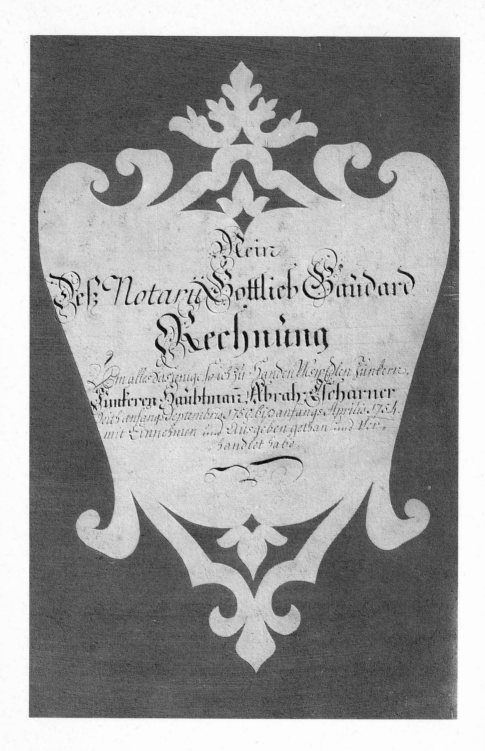

Embellishment on a balance sheet by a Bern notary, Gottlieb Gaudard,
1747. Actual size: 9 inches by 14 inches.

Embellishment on a bequest by the notary, Gottlieb Gaudard, 1753.

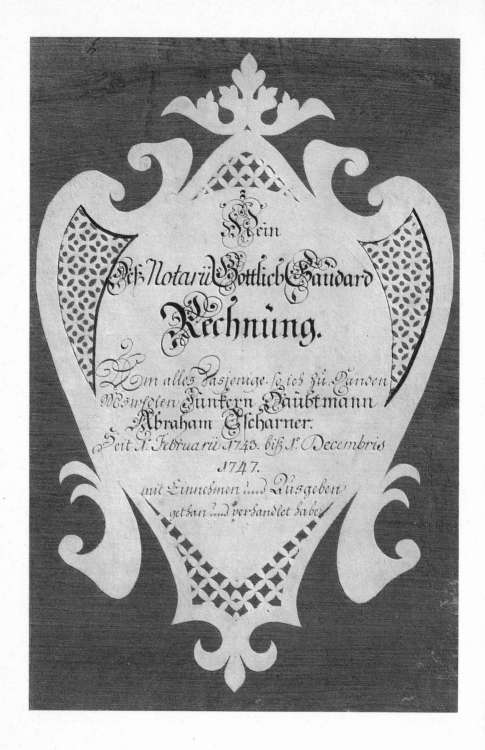

Embellishment on an invoice by Gottlieb Gaudard, 1747. Actual size: $3\frac{3}{4}$ inches by $12\frac{3}{4}$ inches.

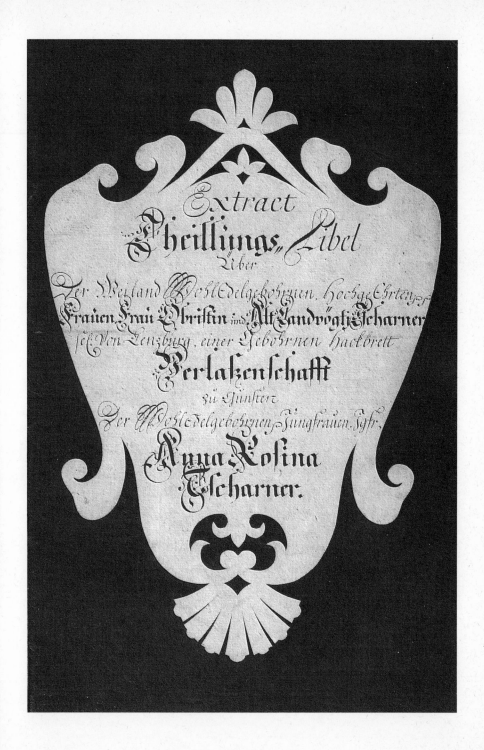

Embellishment on a bequest by Gottlieb Gaudard, 1754. Actual size: 9 inches by 13 inches.

Baroque embellishment on a bequest by a Bern notary named
Wyttenbach, 1772. Actual size: 8 inches by 10 inches.

Embellishment on a bequest by Wyttenbach. A similar basic shape and yet a different decoration. Actual size: $7\frac{1}{2}$ inches by $9\frac{1}{2}$ inches.

Embellishment by Wyttenbach, designed six years later, in 1778. Actual size: $8\frac{1}{4}$ inches by $10\frac{1}{4}$ inches.

FLORAL MOTIFS

Everybody involved in decorative arts finds inspiration in plants and flowers. However, the artist should not try to copy nature. Ornamentation is playing with basic shapes. In paper cutting it means modifying, changing, fitting these shapes into the complete design of the ornament. One basic shape is the rose diamond, with lines that radiate in all directions from the center of the circle. Another is the tulip, with lines running in one direction only from the semicircular base.

Again, do not copy foliage from nature; its purpose is to guide the eye properly within the decorated area. Always try to achieve a balanced and even distribution of the decorative shapes and the cutout areas.

Two of many possibilities in creating decorative tulip shapes. The leaf shapes on the right guide the eye from the base to the main motif.

The tulip base is embellished by adding a "collar."

For this composition a painting on an eighteenth-century chest was adopted. It was simplified and newly designed to fit the available space. The stays on the right were cut off afterward.

Such floral designs are found on many painted household utensils from the
eighteenth century.

This stylized shape of a carnation is very suitable for paper cutting. It can be varied infinitely.

Carnation shape. Leaves guide the eye to the flower.

45

Not an exemplary composition, this nevertheless shows the many possible arrangements achieved by simple cutting.

A more lucid surface design than on the opposite page.

Square cuts require triple folds: first across both axes to make four layers; then diagonally to make eight layers of paper. For further instructions see illustration on top of page 16.

Carnation and tulip shapes arranged this way produce a compact and
restful design in a square area. Note also how the single structures are
connected to each other.

Heart shapes can also be incorporated into floral compositions. Here they should have been made a little larger and divided by cutting out some of the inside area.

The cut on the opposite page has been improved. The heart shapes are larger and their surfaces have been divided according to the design of the other shapes.

51

The center area framed by abundant scrolls is intended for writing, possibly holiday and New Year's greetings. Lettering and scrolls could be done in color.

This cut was folded only once, vertically. It is intended for lettering. The
scrolls could also be painted.

The semicircular cuts along the edge of the heart have been punched out with a round chisel.

The lettering was done and covered with lacquer before cutting was pasted on. Painting was done afterward.

The inspiration for this cut came from a love letter written in 1770 and reproduced in a book entitled *Liebstes Herz, ich bitte dich!* ("Dearest Heart, I Beg You"), in which many old paper cuts are reproduced.

Lettering was done before pasting, and covered with lacquer. The lettering could also have been done using the Roman (see page 79) instead of the Gothic alphabet you see here.

"I am sending you my kind salutations to enter your heart, . . . Buried within your heart in gilt letters." This and similar sayings were written by a man from Emmental, sometime between 1750 and 1800. Actual width: $14\frac{1}{2}$ inches.

Gebet

Herr! schicke, was du
willt,
Ein Liebes oder Leides;
Ich bin vergnügt.
dass beides
Aus deinen Händen
quillt.

Mörike

This new design was inspired by the adjoining cut. Instructions for its preparation are shown in the sketches on the following page. Actual width: 8 inches.

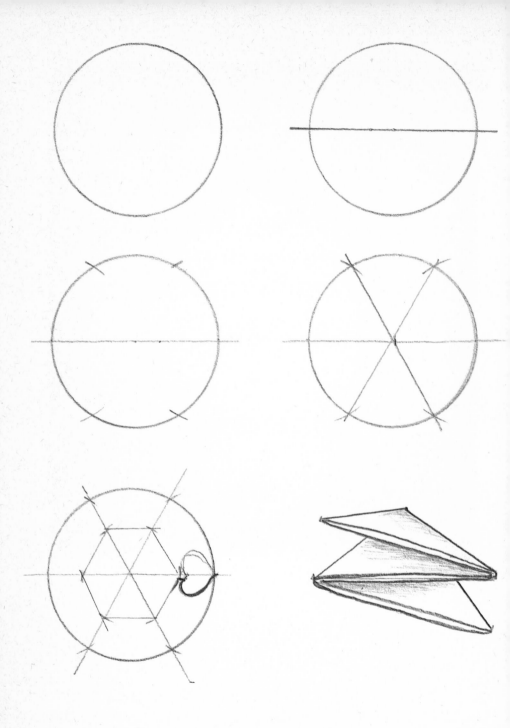

Open compass 4 inches to 5 inches according to size of paper. Divide the circle evenly into six parts, retaining the original diameter, as per drawing. With a pencil draw a hexagon and then a heart shape. Fold accurately according to the sketch.

This cut is adapted from the cut on page 59. The heart shapes start from the sides of the hexagon, instead of the points. This design could also be made into a stencil.

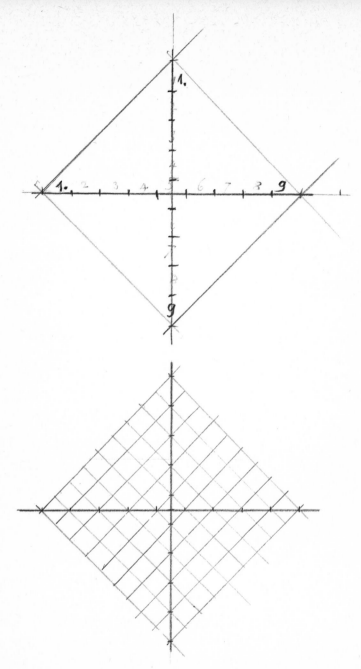

Weavelike patterns, known in Europe for over a thousand years, are particularly suitable for paper cutting. They can be varied infinitely, enlarged, and enriched. Although they may appear to be rather complicated, they are actually easy to construct. Here are a few basic rules: 1. Draw two intersecting lines. 2. Divide each line into nine parts. 3. Connect points one to nine on each side. 4. Draw in parallel lines with a ruler and a triangle. 5. Erase bands to create weavelike pattern. 6. Draw corner loops with compass.

62

It is better to make woven patterns without folding the paper. Cutting can be done quickly after practice. In this example the center bands end up in a point. Most woven ornaments, however, consist of one or more bands without ends (see examples on pages 66 and 67).

64

Floral decorations added to the center bands have made this an attractive structure. It can also be greatly improved by painting and lettering. (Red and blue were used on this piece.)

If you have worked through the preceding examples, this one should be quite easy.

Here the intersecting lines were divided into thirteen parts each.

It is fun to follow the circular writing on the endless woven band. In Truberland, Switzerland, around 1800 even birth certificates were executed in this way.

Here the double curves have been woven into an eight-part circle. The text of the proverb is: "If all of us were rich and everyone were like the other, we would all sit at the table, but who would serve the food?" The construction of this cut is shown on the following pages.

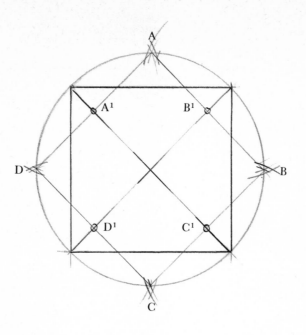

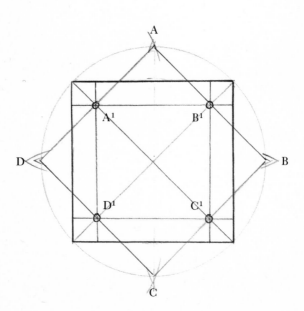

First draw a square with sides about $3\frac{1}{3}$ inches to $3\frac{3}{8}$ inches long. Add diagonals and draw a circle around the square. With the compass, determine the points A, B, C, and D on the circumference of the circle, and draw a square joining these points. Draw the square within a square by connecting points A¹, B¹, C¹, and D¹.

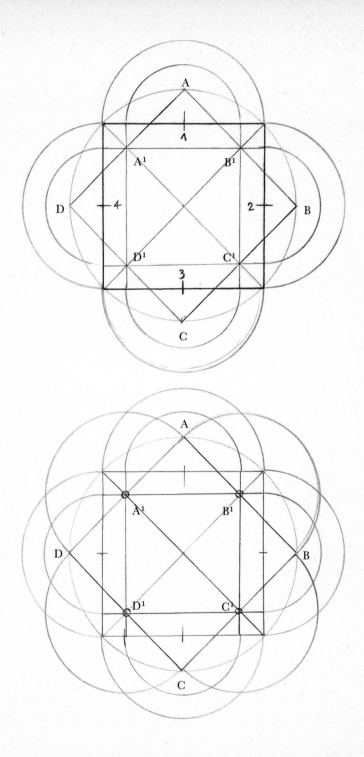

Starting from points 1, 2, 3, 4, draw circular arches. Then draw circular arches starting from points A^1, B^1, C^1, and D^1.

Keep the compass open to point used for the first four inside circles and draw circular arches from points A^1, B^1, C^1, D^1. Now erase the unwanted lines.

There was room for Gottfried Keller's wonderful poem on this endless band arranged in an eight-part circle: "Oh youth, gladly extend your hand to the morrow . . ." On the following pages it is shown how this structure is made.

73

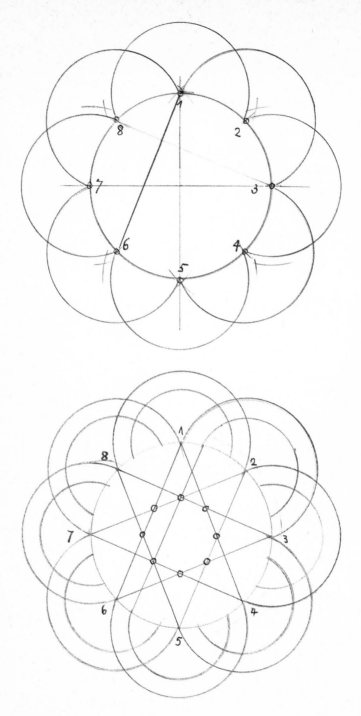

Divide a circle about 7 inches in diameter into eight parts. Draw arches with a compass. Connect points 1 and 6, 1 and 4, 2 and 7, 2 and 5, 3 and 6, 3 and 8, 4 and 1, 4 and 7, etc., with straight lines. (The width of the band will be determined by the intersections on the circle.)

Top: Draw straight lines to connect all the inside curves.
Bottom: Erase for weavelike pattern.

75

Double birds are not only used on coats of arms. They can also bear messages of poetry or greetings. In this folded cut, the semicircular shapes around the heart shape havé been cut out with a hollow chisel.

The dove with an olive branch in its beak is a family emblem in Saanen, Switzerland.

This trellis work was cut out of double-folded paper. The bottom of the bird is a simple, folded cut; the top was cut out of unfolded paper.

78

IJ H L F E T m n

U Y V W P B R S

X Z C D O Q a G

ij r l t f u y h

c e o a d b m n v w

s z ß

Reich immer froh dem Morgen,
O Jugend, deine Hand!
Die Alten mit den Sorgen
Laß auch bestehn im Land!

1 2 3 4 5 6 7 8 9 0

Roman type drawn with a broad pen. Note the guidelines on the fourth
line.

i   d   ſ   t

j   k   ſ   f

n   b   h   ſch

m   ck   s   ß

r   x   ʒ   tz

u

ÿ   das   deſſen   daß

v   flicken fiſchen ſchaffen

w   ſie hatten warten müſſen ~

o   klein aber mein ſoll es ſein

a

g   es iſt ſchlimm, wenn alles

q   bricht und überquillt.

p   plötzlich ſchoß man ſcharf

Gothic type, small letters. Note the three different versions of S, determined by the letter's position in the word.

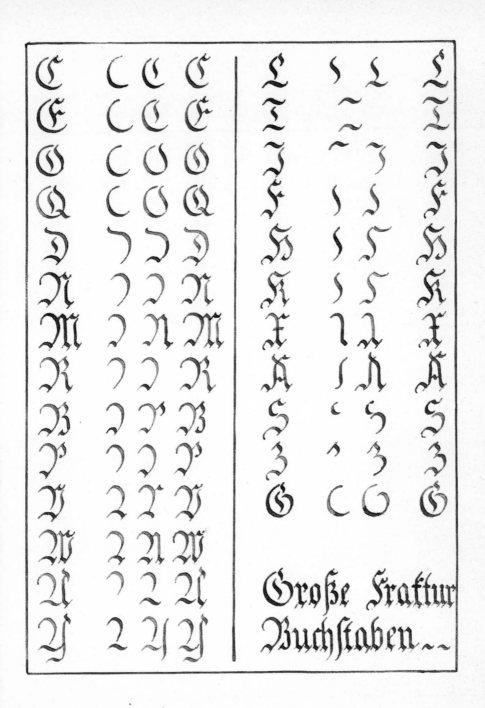

Große Fraktur
Buchstaben...

Gothic type, capital letters. The flourishes require much practice.

Reich immer froh dem Morgen,
O Jugend, deine Hand!
Die Alten mit den Sorgen
Laß auch bestehn im Land!

Reich immer froh dem Morgen,
O Jugend, deine Hand!
Die Alten mit den Sorgen
Laß auch bestehn im Land!

The type face on the bottom is better. Why? Check the guidelines on the
left-hand side. A one-millimeter wide pen was used.

Silhouettes

A silhouette is made by casting a shadow on paper through a reducing apparatus, filling in the shadow with ink, and then cutting it out with scissors and pasting it on a lighter-colored background. Silhouettes of loved ones and of famous people became fashionable in Europe around the middle of the eighteenth century. Even before that, however, ornaments and scenes featuring animals and people were cut out of colored paper. Hand-made paper was particularly favored for this type of paper cutting. In Switzerland paper ornaments were common on birth certificates, love tokens, and New Year's wishes from the beginning of the 1800s. At that time, knives as well as scissors were used for cutting.

It was Johann Jakob Hauswirth (1807–1871) from Saanen in Switzerland who gave the silhouette its own peculiar character and made it famous. He found worthy successors in Louis Saugy (1871–1953) and Christian Schwizgebel (born 1914), both of whom continued his work. Since then artistically inclined men and women all over the world have taken up silhouetting with great enthusiasm.

Making silhouettes is a stimulating and constructive pastime. For the novice it is sufficient to begin with an ordinary pair of scissors. However, the experienced artist may use the special silhouette scissors illustrated below. This device has a long handle and short, pointed cutting edges.

In addition to black paper, colored paper can also be used to produce excellent silhouettes. Here are some fundamental rules:

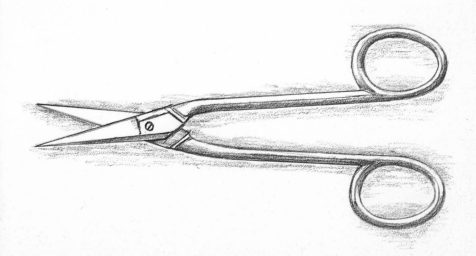

1. It is better to use smooth, thin paper than soft, thick paper.
2. Folded paper should be taped down at loose edges with one or two pieces of adhesive tape.
3. The hand that does the cutting should remain in a static position, while the hand holding the paper moves to form the shape of the silhouette.
4. Start with simple fold cuts and plain, uncomplicated motifs.
5. It is important to repeat the same shapes periodically to improve your technique.
6. A preliminary sketch is often very useful. Do not, however, waste time on details which can be freely executed with the scissors.
7. Work slowly. Become familiar with papers of various qualities and colors. Consider carefully in what size a motif will be most effective.

The young artist Johann Jakob Hauswirth used certain motifs over and over in his silhouettes. Note the shapes of the birds, tulips, and the kind of floral ornamentation.

In his folded cuts Hauswirth always used the same striding horse: practice makes perfect.

Hauswirth used shapes of stags and fir trees for years without any noticeable changes. That is how he became sure of himself.

Here, in a richly designed composition, Hauswirth combined many motifs
which he learned by diligent and continuous practice.

This composition actually consists of two different parts. Hauswirth designed naturalistically, but he did not copy nature. He always depicted fences and garden gates in the same way.

Heart-shaped, vertically folded cut. The chief motifs are bordered by delicate, horizontally guided plant formations.

Much confidence may be gained by varying the same designs. This and
the illustration on the opposite page were done by Johann Hauswirth.

Like Hauswirth, his ideal, Louis Saugy from Rougemont modified a composition he liked again and again. This is how he became a master of the craft.

94

In handicraft as well as in art the experienced master is a dependable and safe guide for the beginner. If the beginning student follows his teacher attentively, he too may soon be able to achieve gratifying results and in time he will become independent and capable of creating his own designs.

95

When Christian Schwizgebel, a native of Saanen, was young he was an Alpine cowherd and an ardent deer keeper. Today nobody is his equal with the scissors. In his pictures he combines naturalistic subjects and embellishments in a masterly fashion. By continuous practice he perfected forms which he uses again and again.

Naturally such a perfect flower design can only be created after much practice. Note the clear distribution of darker paths and delicate scrolls and lattice work. How well the bouquet is set off by empty space against the heart-shaped frame!

In this richly endowed picture with the most minute detail, the division
of the heart shape by horizontal and vertical bands, as well as the ornament
of the fir trees and deer, provide the excitement.

What was said on the opposite page also applies to this design. The attractive variations become apparent when you compare the pictures, which are similar in layout. The compactness of the composition is exemplary.

Slight modifications and there is a new picture. Your confidence to design
has already increased.

100

Section from a larger composition by Christian Schwizgebel. Here you can see the most important rules of silhouette-making: 1. The surface is prominently divided horizontally and vertically. These divisions seem to support the whole structure. 2. Interest is achieved by varying heavy and light shapes. 3. Every part of the surface is well designed.

With silhouettes, it is neither the motifs nor the subjects but the way they are designed and their relationship to each other that are important.

Stencil Painting

Stencil painting is an ancient art, often forgotten but revived again and again. The earliest examples of this ornamental art are ornate, stenciled borders around murals in medieval churches of Switzerland. Pre-Reformation choir stalls in Switzerland are also decorated with stencils.

Stencil paintings came to Europe from the Mohammedan countries of the Orient and North Africa. Arabian-inspired surface ornaments called arabesques were printed in pattern books and popularized throughout Europe. Craftsmen in large cities used thin, wooden arabesques as inlaid designs on furniture. In rural areas, the arabesque pattern was simply transferred to bare wood by painting over it with a blunt brush and thick paint. This technique of stenciling on a design was less expensive than inlaying wood because an existing arabesque could be used again and again on different pieces. In Switzerland and elsewhere in Europe, chests and other household furniture were decorated with arabesque stencils until the end of the seventeenth century.

During the first decade after 1700, multicolored floral ornaments came into wide use in Switzerland, completely replacing the stencil. It regained popularity during the second half of the nineteenth century, when craftsmen started copying ornaments from earlier periods, particularly Gothic and Renaissance. Soon this kind of ornamentation was being done by machine in factories. Borders designed by artists were stamped out hundreds of yards at a time and sold to decorating shops.

Today the art of stenciling is once again properly appreciated because it lends itself so well to surface decoration. The stencil has neither height nor depth but returns the artist, as well as the spectator, to the plane—the foundation for all decorating in color.

HOW IS A STENCIL MADE?

1. Thin, tough, brown paper is most suitable for producing a stencil.
2. If a stencil is coated with thin, clear lacquer it will be more durable and can be used many times because paint cannot penetrate the paper and blur the edges of the design.
3. The only paints suitable for stencil painting are poster colors, slightly diluted. Oil paints, synthetic resin paints, and other similar materials will produce bad or blurred images.
4. The stencil brush, a round brush, cut flat, should be neither too large nor too small. Though a large brush will hold a lot of paint, too much will penetrate under the edges of the stencil, affecting or even ruining the image. If, however, too small a brush is used, the job will take longer.

5. The brush should be cleaned thoroughly with warm water and soap, immediately after use. This is done by pressing the brush with a circular movement against a basin or your palm, then rinsing. Repeat the whole procedure once more with fresh warm water and soap, and, if necessary, wash and rinse several times. Check for paint by spreading the bristles right down to the base. Smooth out brush and store carefully. A dirty brush does not serve well!

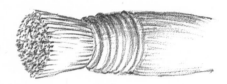

TRANSFERRING THE STENCIL

1. You can transfer a stencil to a foundation of wood, cardboard, or paper. There is no need to prepare the foundation for stenciling.
2. Attach the four corners of the stencil to the foundation with pins or adhesive tape.
3. Dilute sufficient poster paint for stenciling. Mix water and paint in approximately equal quantities. Stir with a flat brush. Do *not* use the stencil brush to stir paint!
4. Place two or three dabs of paint on a separate, small wooden board or cardboard with the flat brush.
5. Dip stencil brush into a dab of paint and turn brush around, holding it in a vertical position so that the tips of the bristles are covered with paint.
6. To distribute paint evenly, make a few short strokes with the stencil brush, still holding it vertical, on another part of the board.
7. Starting from the top left, apply paint to the interstices of the stencil with short, quick strokes, holding brush vertical (see top sketch on page 107). With a knife, press down all edges, particularly tips that protrude.

106

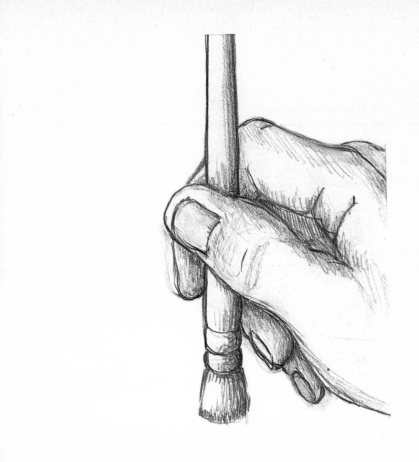

8. When the brush is dry, refill as described in steps 4 through 6. Never dip the stencil brush directly into paint. Always dab new color with the flat brush onto a separate board.
9. Before lifting stencil, check to see that paint has been evenly distributed. If not, dab on additional paint.
10. If after lifting the stencil, you find that paint has seeped under the edges making them blurred, either the paint was too thin or it was not evenly distributed on the brush.

FINISHING THE STENCILED SURFACE

As a rule, the stenciled ornament needs to be framed with a bold outline (see the examples that follow). This is best done with a medium-sized watercolor brush and the ruler shown, which you can construct yourself. This ruler should be about 12 inches long, 1 inch wide and $\frac{1}{4}$ inch thick. The four steel pins used should be $\frac{3}{4}$ inch long.

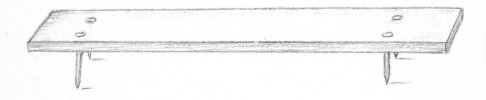

Place the ruler along the border of the stencil and draw a paint-filled brush along the outer edge of the ruler. To keep your hand steady, hold your fourth (ring) finger against the edge of the board as you draw.

FIXING THE STENCIL

It is imperative that you preserve your stencil with fixative. Poster paints are not waterproof and wood foundations, especially fir, are uneven in density. Dirt will accumulate on the stencil over the years, and once it has penetrated to a certain depth, it cannot be removed. There are many good fixatives on the market. After many years of experience, I have found clear lacquer by far the best and easiest material to use. Because it is slow drying, clear lacquer can be applied evenly to the surface. Use a broad, flat lacquer brush and apply clear lacquer with a full brush in long strokes, one next to the other. Draw the brush gently along the edges of the strokes to smooth out any unevenness. Refill your brush and add further strokes. Never rub the unpainted surface with a half-filled brush. Always work quickly and with plenty of lacquer. Once the stencil is fixed, it should be covered with a semigloss lacquer, which contains wax and has a delicate, attractive finish. Semigloss lacquer is also slow drying and spreads easily without getting sticky. Clean your brush immediately after use.

Two or three days later a glaze may be applied over the stencil surface.

PREPARING A TRANSPARENT GLAZE

Transparent glaze is easy to prepare. The following oil paint colors can be used: burnt umber (the effect will be between a smoke color and reddish brown), Van Dyck brown (appears very dark), or burnt sienna (appears very reddish).

1. Squeeze a strip of paint as wide as your finger out of the tube and into a metal or glass cup.
2. Add three to four thimbles of turpentine and stir until dissolved with a flat brush.
3. Add three to four tablespoons of semigloss lacquer and stir with the brush.

It is best to apply glaze to the decorated surface with a special lacquer brush about 2 inches wide. Use a light touch, work carefully, and distribute glaze evenly. Where the edges of the stencil are not clearly delineated, the paint can be wiped off with a rag wrapped around the index finger.

After two or three days, the glazed surface should be covered with another coat of semigloss lacquer.

In the following pages instructions are given for cutting and transferring stencils.

There are two kinds of stencil: 1. a *negative* stencil, in which paper is cut away to form the design; 2. a *positive* stencil, in which the design itself is cut out. In both examples on this page, open space is denoted in gray.

In the negative stencil at the top, spaces are stippled with paint and the shape of the design appears beneath. The pattern at the bottom is a positive stencil.

If you are cutting away the gaps between the shapes and the frame, these have to be attached by "stays" or made sufficiently large so that they touch the outside lines of the frame.

Two negative stencils. The picture at the top is connected to the frame by stays; the picture at the bottom is touching the frame at several points. Both techniques work well.

113

The paper (denoted in black) was folded across both axes. Therefore only one-quarter had to be drawn and cut out.

Slightly diluted color (black) separated this ornament from its frame.
Lines are drawn in with pen on the embracing bands.

The S-shaped basic form is further embellished. This gives the ornament more density and an added interest.

Here, as on page 119, the complete picture is worked over with brush, pen, and slightly diluted paint.

The basic form on page 116 is further embellished.

The protruding tips must be held down with the point of a knife when transferring this cut.

Note center design of this doublefold cut.

All kinds of lines were added to this negative stencil with a pointed brush and diluted paint.

Delicate shapes were added to the large basic form of this doublefold cut.

Actually *one* stay would have sufficed between the curled leaf of each quarter and the center section. This four-part fan now acts as an ornamentation.

Square, four-part folded cut, executed by a thirteen-year-old. He used
three motifs: the heart shape, the tulip, and the curled leaf.

The tracks of the stays between the curled leaves, the tulips, and the heart shapes were covered with diluted paint afterward. Note the additional embellishments on particular shapes.

A singlefold cut. The basic layout is a large flower shape, the wavy blade of a lance, and a curled leaf. The ornament is connected to the frame in appropriate places.

The same ornament has been detached from its frame and made independent with a narrow stroke of the brush.

Modifications, enrichments, or simplifications of a basic design are instructive exercises for the student of decorative arts. Here the pair of leaves under the flower shape has been made heavier than in the design on page 126.

The isolated, stiff-looking pair of leaves under the flower shape has a disturbing effect on the complete picture.

It is easier to adorn a squat rectangle with few motifs. The fan-shaped
flower dominates the area. (Compare with design on page 126.)

130

Here good balance is maintained between dark and light surfaces. This composition is better than the one on page 127.

The principal shapes of a floral ornament should not guide the eye beyond the decorated area. Therefore the curled leaf is a useful motif.

One can produce a balanced ornament with bold, principal shapes and small additions in the right places. The light, overall area should be larger than the dark one.

A compass-created, circular shape should not be cut out of folded paper.
Here is a positive stencil where the picture has been cut out. It contains
twelve curved motifs drawn with the compass.

The twelve curved shapes should have been made a little larger to run closer to the outside curves. The picture would have been more interesting if these were cut narrower.

Here what was criticized in the picture on page 135 has been taken partly
into account.

The stencil is now fuller and more satisfying than the one on page 135.
The framing arches, however, could still be narrower and positioned a
little closer to the ends.

This hexagonal cut was constructed with the compass. Original diameter was $7\frac{1}{4}$ inches. The inside rose diamond was constructed first, then the outside arches were added. The different arches were done by shifting positions of the compass.

Stencil pictures may also be done in several colors. Here a richer, more colorful image was achieved by adding decorative red lines with brush and pen.

Eight-part circular ornament, also constructed with the compass. Note the few attachments to surrounding border. The round holes in the outside leaf shapes were punched out with a circular chisel.

Dots and lines were drawn in with a fine pen and compass on this red ornament. Diameter of the original picture: $7\frac{1}{4}$ inches.

Note the rich effect of this trellis work arranged inside a six-part circle. Its construction with the compass is easier than you think: draw arches over the six main circles, opening the compass wider each time. (See page 60 for a similar design.)

142

Just a few red dots and lines were added to the trellis work, creating a polychromatic effect. The same cut was used in the composition shown on page 166.

This cut is similar to the one shown on page 124. The principal motifs of tulip, heart, and curled leaf are larger, producing a more compact design and diminishing the dark areas.

Two hues, reddish brown and yellow green, cover the light ornament. The transparent oil color glazes described on page 109 are used. Before applying glaze the ornament is covered with clear lacquer. A similar effect could also be obtained by using diluted poster paints or watercolors. In this case a previous covering with clear lacquer would be unnecessary.

Freely shaped animals may easily be included as principal or secondary motifs. Here again, a singlefold cut has been used to achieve balance in this ornament. By floral designs in the background the eye returns to the center of the picture.

This glaze was applied here with fast and free strokes. A more abundant and stronger border would probably have improved the effect of the picture. Compare the cut with the stencil and you will notice that the disturbing crosspieces around the birds' wings and feet have been covered.

When incorporating a swan motif inside an upright rectangle, a counter balance is needed. Here a freely designed carnation shape has been chosen.

This border is more forceful than the one in the stencil on page 147.

Copy of a positive stencil made in 1726.

The transfer of this cut was done in three colors: 1. The circular shape was covered with dark gray poster paint and then the cut was carefully attached to it. 2. Yellowish gray color was stippled on. Border lines were protected by paper strips. 3. The ruby-colored paint was added. Again borders were covered up with paper strips. The circular lines of the frame were drawn in with the compass.

This design was found on a church bench painting from the second half of the seventeenth century in Bern.

152

Development of this picture: 1. Application of dark gray foundation.
2. Stippling on the red. 3. Adding the green. Framing was done with the
drawing pen.

153

Coat of arms and shield bearer on the choir bench of a family named
Sprecher, found in the church of Luzein in Grisons, Switzerland, and
dating from the year 1670. Above is a copy of the coat of arms.

154

A few years ago the stencil painting on the choir bench of Luzein was "restored." In the process, its original character was obliterated by over-painting the spaces between the stays. Since this was done freehand, the sharp cutting edges were also lost. *Note:* When restoring damaged, old stencil paintings, exact copy cuts are essential.

A sector of stencil painting in the church of Jegenstorf (canton Bern) from
the year 1655. Actual width: $14\frac{7}{8}$ inches. Band ornament in Renaissance
style is also found on chest paintings of that period.

In its permanent position this stencil picture is, of course, surrounded by wooden architecture. The bands of the arabesque ornament are designed in such a way that the eye never glides beyond the decorated area. The curled ends act as anchorage points.

Copy of Grisons chest painting from the second half of the seventeenth century. Original size: 14 inches by $11\frac{1}{4}$ inches.

The paneling on this chest is rectangular, but nevertheless the Baroque
ornament in the Roman arch is a suitable design.

Negative stencil painting from a Grisons chest from the second half of the
seventeenth century.

In this positive stencil painting the decorated shapes were colored and not the spaces. Actual size: $15\frac{1}{2}$ inches by $11\frac{1}{4}$ inches.

161

Cut after a stencil painting on a chest in upper Emmental, from the year 1706. The decoration on this chest was badly damaged and a new cut was required. Actual size: $12\frac{1}{2}$ inches by $8\frac{3}{4}$ inches.

The background of this stencil painting was done in a brick red. The surrounding bands and painting are also in the style of the original. Size of the panel: $16\frac{1}{2}$ inches by $12\frac{3}{4}$ inches.

Cut after a stencil painting on a chest from Simmental, done in the
second half of the seventeenth century. This, too, was restored. Actual
size: $15\frac{1}{2}$ inches by 9 inches.

The negative stencil was transferred to the red background. The stays in this arched ornament look genuine. Roman arches and rectangles go well together.

Here two different ornamental styles have been used to adorn a rectangular area.

STENCIL PAINTING LETTERS AND NUMERALS

In stencil painting, as in other techniques for ornamentation, lettering and dates should fit harmoniously into the design. This means that they, too, have to be cut and then transferred to background with a rounded brush. By far the most suitable type of lettering is the Roman alphabet. On the following pages, the complete Roman alphabet is shown. Note the relationship of width and height in each letter.

For technical reasons the cut letters, too, have to have stays.

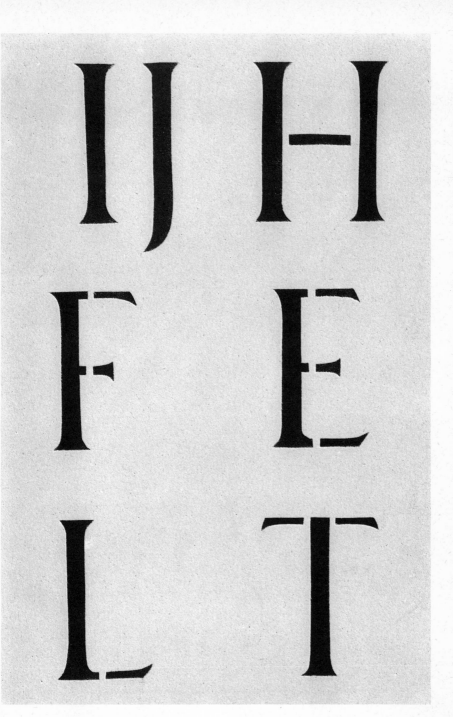

As a rule the marks of the stay are covered with paint afterward.

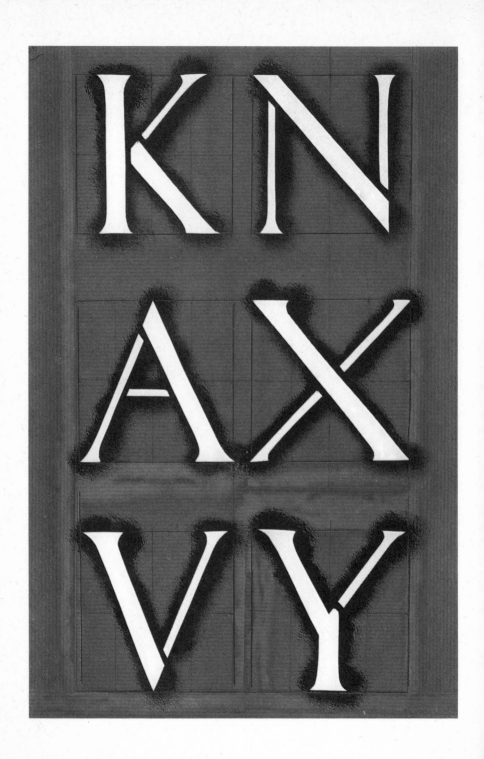

As the pencil marks reveal, all letters were constructed on the basis of a square.

170

The bars slanting to the right must be at least double the width of the ones slanting to the left.

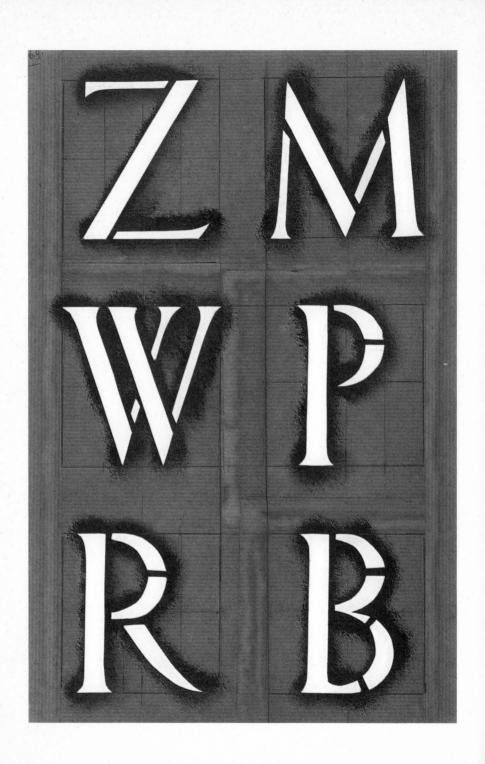

Here, too, the square is used as the basis for the letter shape.

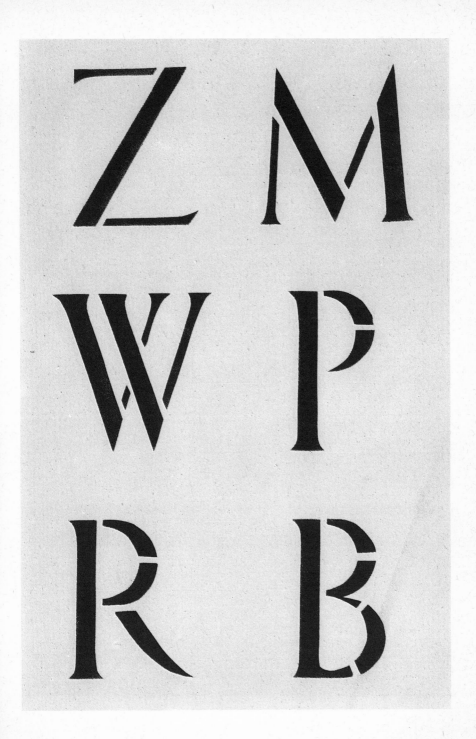

With P, R, and B, the track marks interfere with the image of the letters. Therefore, an improvement is called for.

The outside of the O may be drawn with the compass. For the other
letters depicted above, this tool may also be used.

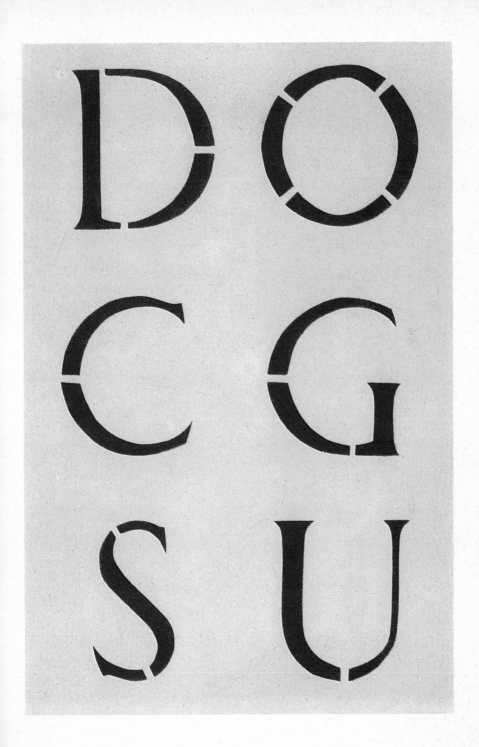

With the D, the arch joining the perpendicular must be made wider at
the bottom.

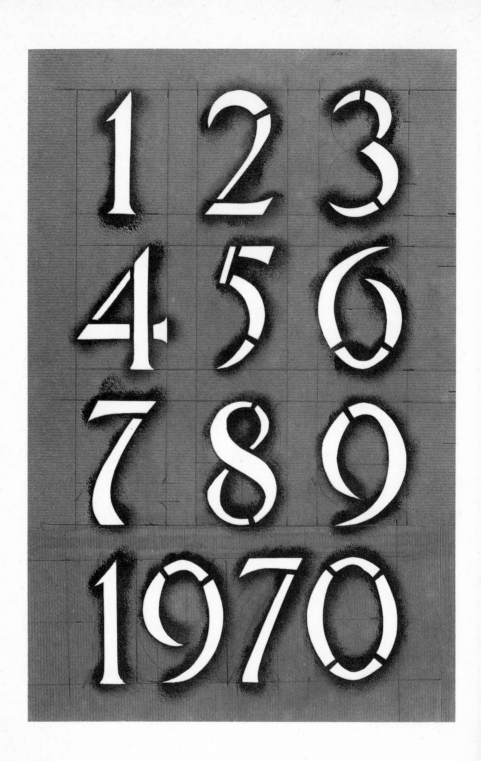

In sixteenth- and seventeenth-century prints you will find good examples of Arabic numerals.

Here it is advisable to cover up the track marks. The bottom part of the 7 was made a little too wide.